Hidden Place

Mwihaki Kiiru

 ISBN: 979-8-9851736-0-4(Paperback)
979-8-9851736-1-1(eBook)

Library of Congress Control Number: 2021922807

Cover Design by Mwihaki Kiiru
Cover Art Designed in Canva
Interior Designs by Audrey Farrell
Author Images by Abigail Bailey
Printed by Mwihaki Kiiru in the United States of America.

First printing edition 2021.

[thehakimanagement@gmail.com]

Dedication

My Creator above (God)
- You've seen me through and through.
  I'd be nothing without you. All Glory.

My creator below (Mom):
- I am because you are. Thank you, Lord, for activating the definition of strength in human form and enabling me to be a first-hand witness. My rock. I love you mama.

Cole (Collette)
- Angel above, I miss you. Thank you.

Contents

Contents

Preface

This pain gave me the most beautiful gift. One that I can only repay by releasing all the tears, doubts, sleepless nights, worthless fights, mind spirals, and the joyful moments of understanding. A gift that I can send to a new rightful location. Now tying it with a ribbon of forgiveness and sealing it with a sleeve of love. In the hopes of bringing the new owner the clarity I found in my time of turmoil, gratitude I found in the midst of uncertainty, and the love and answers I found within.

My gift is soil. Your gift is to plant. Plant with purpose so your gift may soon become the moon in one's darkness or the rays to one's sun.

Enjoy the *Hidden Place* soundtrack,
songs written, sung, and composed by the author.
The link can be found at iamhaki.com.

Hidden Place

1. signatures

Signature 1

I faked a smile as if I had turned plastic.
I knew I couldn't feel because the repercussions would be drastic.

When I spoke, was my voice heard?

Looking back, my voice was used as my disguise,
Singing was the only aspect of my voice that represented me
without scaring you.

I compromised my safe haven and turned it into my shield.
Come to me when you need, it said, but keep your lips sealed.

I suffocated for so long I forgot how to breathe.
Once I left, I questioned if my identity was still underneath.

Lost in this suppressed aggression,
Ashamed of my newly found confession.
Would I ever revert to the original composition?
Or had I already compromised my being by being

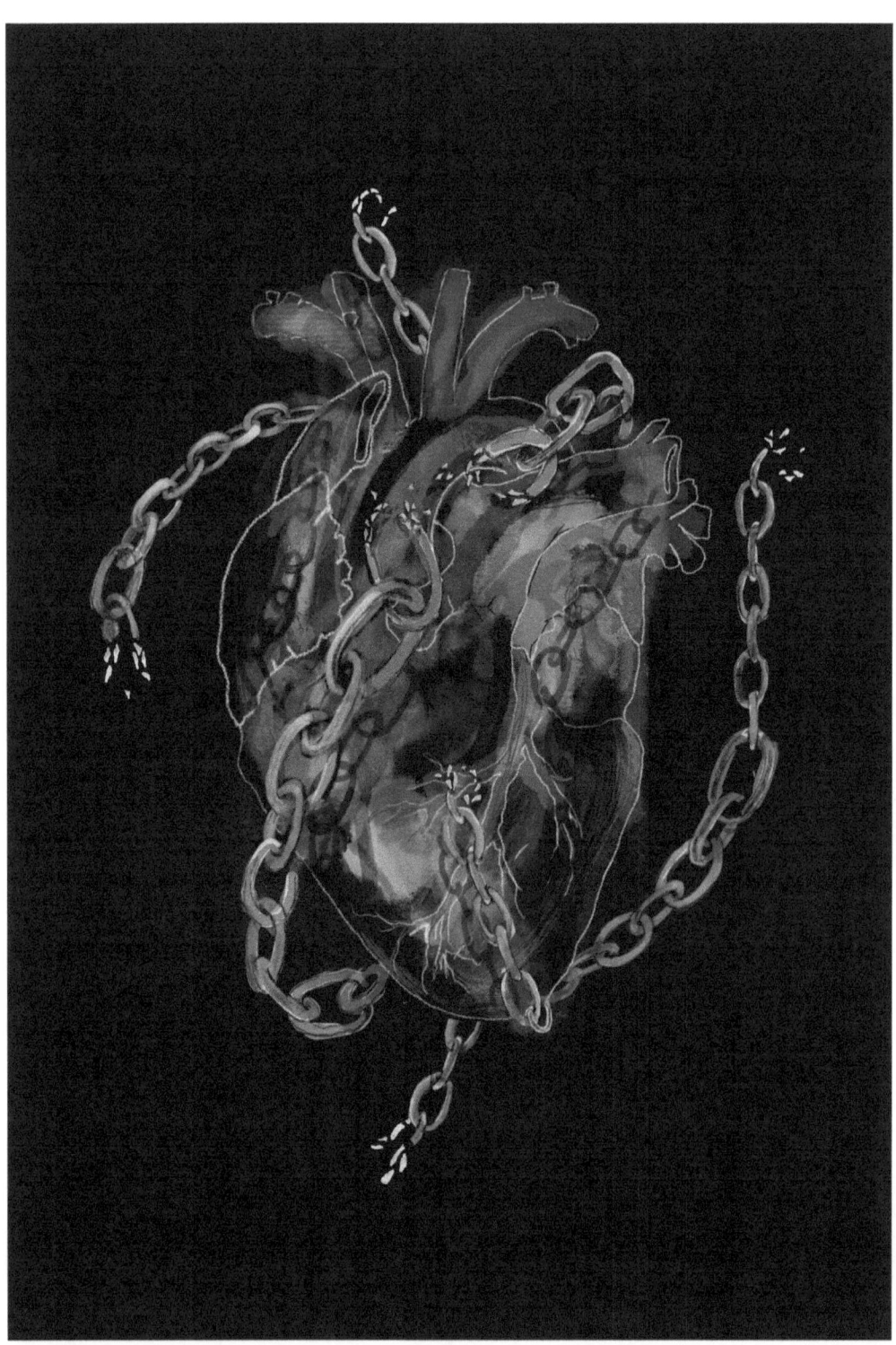

Cut It

You go the hardest for me for the media,
Yet treat me the worst when it's home and it's me N ya.

Tired of always waiting for you to change,
Cry when I call you out then you switch up the blame.

Said you were sorry, and you understood,
Thought this relationship would switch for the good.

So, time and time I said nah, you didn't mean that,
Ignored my intuition just to feed that,
Part of me that was used to the pain,
Till I realized there is nothing I'd gain.

Love your significant and send love to others.
Love to your sister, your mother, your brother.
But don't get it twisted, we all hurt each other
When it's those you love it's just undercover.

See one holds the knife and one reaps the cut,
One takes longer to heal one takes a shorter cut
Of breaking boundaries without giving a fuck,
A vampire using another neck to suck.

But it's my fault for giving you the benefit which would form
all these doubts,
Addicted to taking the love I'd give out.
I ain't no sign-up sheet, I ain't no Girl Scout,
Putting two fingers up to promise I'm pledging out.

But I know you did it because you weren't healed.
Tried to grab my flame, you needed something to feel.
In the midst I got lost in your insecurities,
Which made me believe I wasn't secure in me.

Just because I love you and leave don't mean it don't hurt,
But I did this for me, I needed to search
For the same love I was giving to you
That you took for granted and used to abuse.

Let's say what it was, it was toxic.
Adventitious way to try and shoplift,
Took my picture then decided to crop it,
Queued the violin, now I've decided to stop it.

So, this ain't no whatchu talkin' about Willis,
Accept in one way that you were the villain.
Yea you took my brush to paint different strokes,
But still I rise. Word to Ms. Angelou.

Interlude 1.

I was drowning, yet no one could see how far I had gone.

I'd stare in the mirror and be frightened by my reflection.
I no longer recognized myself.

I would see the sun underwater, but no matter how fast I'd swim
up,
It felt like I was just getting further away and more tired.

I had cried more than I did in ten years.
I had become so familiar with the feeling of pain mentally and
physically that when I got ten minutes of absolute tranquility,
I'd lie still, feel the warm tears fall down my face and think of
what it would be like to keep this feeling for just an extra five
minutes or even at least for the day.

I'd lie there and yearn for the freedom I once had.

In a way, I felt as if I was being punished or was incarcerated for
a crime I hadn't committed. I had pleaded not guilty for so long,
but since I loathed this feeling, I chose the shorter sentence by now
pleading guilty.

So, what if I made a false claim?
At least I'd receive a shorter sentence and have a better chance of
saving myself before I'd hit the bottom.

My mind, body, and spirit had their own quiet breakup.
At first the split was amicable. Until each one learned
they could no longer live without the other, yet no one would
cave and say so.
In this case, I was forced to comply with their decision.

I guess the easiest way to explain the silent and sudden breach
was that I had lost control. And whatever fate awaited, I would
have to be okay, even if I had no say.

Follow the Leader

Where do we run when fear follows?

When it slowly becomes your shadow,

Do you hide and pray that it seeks somewhere else?

Or do you play tag and run like hell
....

I hated to admit that it wrapped around me like a weighted blanket,

Some days were better than others, some nights were more painful.

I would remind myself it was only temporary. And hoped to make it through the night.

"Please stop shaking," "breathe," while anxiously thinking about how I even got here.

When did all this get so bad?
  .....

Days turned into weeks and weeks into months,

Yet every day started to blend in with one another.

It was like staring at a sheet of white paper
Or being featured in one of those movies
where you relive each day until you get it right.

I don't know who made these rules, but how could I even get it "right" if I wasn't even sure how I got it wrong?
  ....

At first, I'd look for the answers in all the wrong places,

Until one day I decided to take a long, long walk, and asked "it" to come along.

Interlude 2

I knew I had reached a dangerous place when other people wanted it more for me than me.

The one thing that had kept me going for all these years was slowly dissipating, yet I was too tired to even acknowledge it.

Internal/External

We learn a lot from our struggle
And even more through our troubles.
Tirelessly rummaging through our recollection,
To see where it all began.
Helplessly seeking our yellow brick road,
While clasping to the idea that there is still that pot of gold.

The process can be long and gruesome,
Rewarding when you learn you grew some,
While saying fuck you,
To the man who said you'd never bloom son.
Trust.

Days spent looking at the empty night in fury,
Mornings spent looking at the morning sky with gratitude,
It's a cycle.

But I learned to ride,
Adjusted with every high tide,
Took every punch they struck to my left eye,
Stood firm in me and revitalized
Even when I felt stuck inside, I could not compromise
I had gone too far.

So, when I chase the sun,
It is because I need to,
It is my closest thing to freedom,
It is the only life I have ever known.

Interlude 3

Faith became my tranquilizer

The day I realized

I had nothing more to give.

Past Participles

How are you going to say you want the old me back,
Don't you understand that I miss her too?
Her smile, her kind eyes, looking at the world with surprise,
Her gentle soul, before it was swallowed whole,
Then enveloped by the world's edge, giving her a paper cut.

Or so she had thought.....

Wired to Rewire

See that's the thing they never tell you about growth
Our minds are programmed to think we have made an oath,
To our old selves,
Old patterns,
Old friends.

But old... that's just what it is,
And at what cost is this false information sold?

A facade of debilitating practices
Wrapped in red ribbon,
Ready to unravel the second you say,
"Hey wait a minute."
Then boom!
There goes all your shit,
Coming out of the box, like the storage closet your mom never opens.

To be frank, it's rigged.
Our control system tells us one thing
And when we decode the operating system and rewire it,
We now begin fighting a civil war.
Past beliefs = South,
And the present: knowledge, evolution, freedom = North.

In the end,
We know which one wins,
Yet, the choice is yours.
Pick your opponent.

23

A Beautiful Place where Nothing Grows

Cheers to being less authentic and more to following trends.
That's what's celebrated,
Domino effect once our insecurities are exacerbated
By society's perception,
Media's deception,
Just another vault for subreption,
So don't get it twisted on common misconceptions

Let me give you Tupacets of advice—
You either grow or you disappear,
You either change or you live in fear.
My proclamation:
"Emancipate your mind from the shackles of societal influence.
Become fluent in the idea of individuality rather than commonality."

It is about time this fair use principle is abolished.

Refugee

If I could,
I would run away from the world,
From the mass destruction,
From humanity's obedience,
In order to avoid the debris from our own deficiency,
Compassion.

My most common ally would be my reflection.
My most trusted companion would be my shadow.
And my most treasured confidant would be my pen and paper.

If I could,
I would run away from the world,
So I could learn to breathe again.

Dream Deferred 2

What happens to a dream deferred?
- *Langston Hughes*

A dream deferred is far worse than being
deferred from college,
As if you willingly choose to bury your ancestor's knowledge.
The truth in your soul is unable to grow,
The seeds planted are that of fears,
Watered by lament and tears
Left to wither on the windowsill
As you watch at your own will.

A dream deferred is far worse than being
deferred from college,
Because you blatantly acknowledged
That your soul's purpose would be put on hold just to be
demolished.

Fighting Fear with Fear

Fear not evolving,
Fear reaping the effect of when your mind
chooses to stop transforming.
When the universe no longer knocks at your door
because she's grown weary of trying for too long
and too hard only to be answered by a fist
hitting the wall signaling her to "shut up" or "go away."
Fear emerging out of the consciousness of your human state
and re-emerging and ascending to heaven's floodgates
to be asked the daunting yet highly anticipated question,
"What did you do with all that I gave you?"

So be anything but scared of growth,
But fear never coming face to face with what stunted that growth,
You.

Caged Bird

Now I understand just why the caged bird sings,

Or maybe I just grasp how the caged bird thinks....

Middle Seat

Passengers on the same train
Waiting for our stop,
Not knowing our destination or location.

Crazy to think we were placed on the same ride at the same time,
Yet at different moments. But, regardless, we arrived.

I look to my left and see a familiar face.
I walk over and sit to converse.
What is your story?

I look to my right and see someone who looks like my mom,
I send a warm smile and invite her to sit.
What is your story?

Each story, different yet intertwined,
Everyone, inherently unique and perfect by design.

Wish for You

I watch as kids run on the playground and swing on the swings
As their parents push them high enough to touch their dreams

My hope would be to keep them young just for a little longer
Or as long as it takes to help them believe that they are stronger

Than what life throws and the challenges that await
To remind them that life is truly based on the happiness you create

So, as I hear them laugh, I pray in ten years they hear that same echo
To keep swinging on those swings and to never ever let go

That is what we call the game of life,
One day you are being pushed closer and closer to the sun
And the next you turn back to realize you are the only one

No push or pull to propel you closer to your dreams
Except the inner voice in your mind that whispers
"By any means"

3. Hidden Place

Hidden Place

Happiness, the feeling we are all searching for,

The state that can feel the most comfortable,
Yet at times, the most unfamiliar.

The most inviting place yet the most unwelcome,

The "easiest" route yet the road less traveled.

The solution to the problem, yet the hardest to calculate.

The GPS to freedom, yet the most complicated to navigate.

Why is that?

Maybe what we are searching for is hidden under the things
we buried long ago.
Which is why the thought of acquiring it seems so distant or
unfamiliar.

Some say the things buried were needed to shift into survival
mode.

But what happens when you no longer must survive in that "mode,"

When you no longer must carry the heavy load,

When all that is left is the same wonderful being created from the start?

Yet, naturally a little more bewildered and sheltered

You have been through things, you are older, and the world looks a little different than you remember.

Or,

You are so used to your guard being up you are almost scared to see what is behind.

So, yes, things are different,

But different is not a bad thing.

In this case, call it a rebirth, a second chance.

Now, your only responsibility is to simply unpack,
One layer at a time.

That of pain, grief, anger, strife, anxiety, depression, stress and despair, and with each layer unpacked, sending a letter off back to where it belongs.

For example:

Anxiety,

"You were one of the most uncomfortable motherfuckers to live with. You were not considerate when you saw I was busy, either. We often fought when it was time to go out and enjoy my day, and frankly you were quite messy in general. You would enter the room just as cool as you please, and often just to disturb my peace. The irony in it is I got used to your ass. You no longer became an intruder. Rather, I looked at you as more of a crooked Santa Clause. I had become so used to you taking the cookies that I now offered you a glass of milk to wash them down when you were done. We had a long run and although the fun was one sided, you taught me a lot. However, your reign is over."

So, with each sendoff that feeling, the feeling we're all searching for, that had once become unfamiliar, slowly becomes familiar again.

In the midst you gladly accept its invitation and elongate your stay.

It is then you open your eyes only to find your old footprints, on the road less traveled,

And to realize your calculations were correct this whole time, you just solved for Y rather than X-Ing out all the extra baggage.

But it is okay because it happens to... all of us.

When you look within your *Hidden Place* sometimes by will and at times by force, you find that under all that clutter was the feeling that you were searching for all along.

In a way by unpacking, each layer had become the roadmap.

It is when we accept our quest to our *Hidden Place*, daunting yet the most rewarding,

That we truly find fulfillment.

Maze Runner

C c o g g n i t t e l g n i t p e c c a
o o e l g n i t p e c c a g n i t n g
n n t r f n o c o g g n i t t o n
f f t o c a g n i t n o r f n o c e r i
r r i n c n i t n o r f n o c o l f t
o o n t e g a c c e p t in gl e o g g n n
n n g i p t t i n g l e t t i n g g n o o
t t g n g a c c e p t in g lett i n i c r
i i o c o n f r o n t i n g a c c e p t o f
n n g a c c e p t in g l e t t i n g g n
g a c c e p t i n g l e t t i n g g o c o
(confronting, accepting, letting go)

40

Glory

I heard His voice in the crossfire.
In the stillness of dawn,
It travelled through the Serengeti
And found its way back to me,
It was not too late—
"This is where I wanted you to be."
My restoration was found through repentance then acceptance,

For I had wandered far beneath wishes
And high above the depths
To my own confrontation.

This face,
My face,
A face I had seen many times
But through a different lens,
Was reborn again.

Signature 2

Severed ties, underlying lies,
Pain buried, behind big brown eyes.
Smile so wide she forgot how to
cry,
Fear becoming second nature,
Knowing no one could save her.

Her heart, a jar
of honey,
Left ajar to the
love that she
needs,
A yellow rose
in a field of
weeds,

A seed, ready to plant her tree,
In search of her hidden key.

But Baby Girl,

It is time to be selfish.

And when I cry, laugh, sing you ought to bet imma' belt it.

That is my black joy,

That is my choice,

That is my voice.

Let what is in come without

An ounce of shame,

A relief from strain,

All aboard!

This ride is express

Conveyer belt to the next

Chapter of growth, chapter of love,

Making a toast to my fam up above,

This is my time to boast about my ancestor's love.

Thank you for this knowledge, my joy, my gifts,

For unlocking fear that hindered my shifts.

Grateful to say the least, pure bliss when my mind is at peace,

With myself, with others, with my enemies, with God.

I Am

I am the master of my own self-discovery,
In the process of myself recovery,
Inhaling the world's wisdom and exhaling every ounce of despair,
Recognizing my capabilities,
Extending my horizon,
Admiring each season that presents growth
While reflecting and accepting past mistakes.

I remind myself of what I already know.

My mind has preconceived the dreams I envision,
And my eyes are now fixed to its destination,
A destination that has long awaited
To be nurtured,
To be manifested,
To be.

I remind myself of what I already know.

To the fears that once attempted to block my success,
I now greet you with my resilience,
My newfound strength.
I find warmth in my discomfort,
I find happiness in my curiosity,
I find serenity in my creativity,
I have found love through my independence.

What is most magical is the truth that laid here all along
What is most painful is the latency to recognize it in yourself.
This knowledge
A knowledge I deem as gratuitous, a guileless whisper,
A congenial delicacy, a fortuitous treasure.
Beautiful, rare and in some way ancient
Waiting for its revival, ready to be awoken.

Fly Little Blackbird

If I searched for hours
Then searched for days
To find the mystery
Of the game we all play

And If lost myself
Doing just that then
What would it all mean
If I never make it back

So I say

Fly little blackbird
Don't let them clip your wings
I know you're tired of falling
But the message we must bring
So don't cry little blackbird
You'll soon understand why
Your world is crumbling on your journey to the sky

So just fly little black bird
And don't you look down
Ohhh destiny's calling
Just follow the sound

Bonus Content

The Rose that Grew from Concrete pt.2

Beautiful girl,
Who lived in her world,

Learned to breathe fresh air
By following dreams,
When odds would compete
She didn't care.

Learned life isn't fair,
But she would not dare
Let that hold her back.

Because she was the rose,
Waiting to unfold
Between the worlds crack in the concrete.

Ohh who would she be,
The rose in the concrete,
Who learned to walk without no feet
The rose in the concrete,
Ohh wait till the world sees,
Ohh who would she be,
The rose that grew from the concrete.

Just the
Beginning ...

Rise

Block your blessings while I stand in the shadow
Pulled a fast one I choose my battles
I walk away when snake starts to rattle
And close the gate when dusk starts to settle

Don't cower away from those who talk behind
You choose your bed and I choose to lie
Face up and mind towards the sky
To the one who blesses my life ohh

Proud of you baby

Meet The Author

Where we walk we don't see the endless possibilities
Of who we are and were created to be
Yet we roam a tundra with the belief we're free
What it's like to walk blindly and to never know,
To reach for stars you are told may never glow
To hide the special cards you are told to never show
To man with the untrained eye you are just as valuable as fools gold
To man with an untrained mouth it is easy to believe
false information sold
To man with an untrained nose do not mistake this virus for a cold
To man with an untrained ear be careful resonating with the lies
you're told
To man with a heart turned cold, do not place the burden of your
severed dream on a starving soul

                                            - Mwihaki Kiiru

Author's Note

To this book:
Thank you, for finding your way to me. You came at a time when I needed you most.

To my readers:
Thank you for reading and now coming on this journey with me.

My poetry is the telescope view to my soul. So, welcome.

Chapter 1. Signatures:
Is a chapter that refers to the involuntary signatures I gave away.
Chapter 2. Thoughts Processed:
This chapter stems from the myriad of new ideas that I resonated with.
Chapter 3. Hidden Place:
Essentially the book's title speaks for itself.
'Signature 2' in Chapter 3, is my final signature.

References

Angelou, Maya. *I Know Why the Caged Bird Sings*. Ballantine, 2015.

Frost, Robert, Louis Untermeyer, and Robert Frost. *The Road Not Taken: A Selection of Robert Frost's Poems*. New York: H. Holt and Co, 1991. Print.

Hughes, Langston. "Harlem" from *The Collected Works of Langston Hughes*. Copyright © 2002 by Langston Hughes.

Shakur,Tupac Amaru. "The Rose That Grew From Concrete." *The Rose That Grew from Concrete*, Pocket, London, 2006.

Simone, Nina. "Blackbird."Blackbird / Little Liza Jane . Coplix, 1963. Vinyl.

www.ingramcontent.com/pod-product-compliance
Lightning Source LLC
Chambersburg PA
CBHW051552120626
46551CB00013B/1490